Jeff Bowick & Dwayne Henriksen

TRADING STRATEGIES AND SECRETS:

DAY TRADING SCALPING SWING TRADING

All you have to know about the short-term strategies of Day Trading, Scalping and Swing Trading

Table of Contents

INTRODUCTION

Short-term trading strategies are among the most widely used methods to take advantage of smaller market movements than traditional investments.

When trading short term you take a position that can last from a few seconds to several days. It is used as an alternative to the more traditional buy and hold strategy, where you hold a position for weeks, months or even years.

Short-term trading focuses primarily on price movement, rather than the long-term fundamentals of an asset. This style of trading seeks to take advantage of rapid market price movements and thus identifies market volatility around key economic data, corporate earnings and political events.

Short-term trading is also referred to as active trading, as it differs greatly from the investment or passive fund trading strategy. It is generally based on speculation, which means that it does not have to involve buying and selling the underlying assets. In contrast, short-term traders tend to favor derivative instruments, which means they can open and close positions without having to own the underlying asset.

To start short term trading, it is good to:

- Choose what type of short-term trader you intend to be.
- Identify the markets for short-term trading.

- Choose a short-term trading strategy.

- Practice using your strategy with a demo account.

- Open an account to trade in real markets.

What are the types of short-term traders?

There is a wide range of different styles that short term traders can choose from, depending on their time constraints and risk appetite. The types analyzed are:

Day trader

Scalper

Swing trader

There are various markets in which short-term trading is possible. The trading style places few constraints on the duration for which a position is held open (from a few seconds to several weeks), so that the opening time of a market need not impact the chosen methodology. Ultimately, the choice made will be based on personal preferences and interests.

The most commonly used markets for short-term trading are:

Forex

Stocks

Indexes

Cryptocurrencies

Commodities

Now that we've done the proper introduction, let's move on to look specifically at the different types of short-term trading.

DAY TRADING

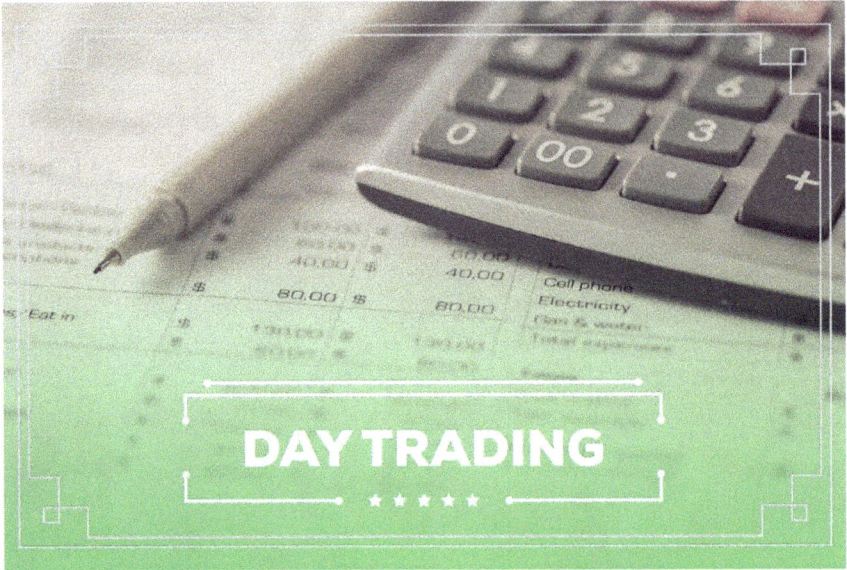

Also known as "shorting," this is by far one of the most popular kinds of trading in America today. When a trader chooses to "day trade," they are simply going to be buying and selling financial instruments (such as stocks) on the same day. In other words, they are not holding onto an instrument for any extended period of time.

Day trading is a style of investing that requires you to buy and sell stocks or forex on the same day. Most trades are made within the course of a day, though some strategies require you to hold onto your investments for several days or longer. No matter how long you're holding onto your trade, the goal of day trading is still the same: making trades based on market trends and making trades as quickly as possible to maximize profit. Day trading does not necessitate that you take advantage of short-term fluctuations in the market. You can day trade anything with a high volatility and reliable price movement, such as foreign currencies or individual stock issues.

Most day traders use some sort of automated trading platform to keep track of their trades. Many forex and futures brokers offer trading software, though it's typically built for more advanced investors. For stocks, there are a number of great apps to help you invest all from your phone or computer. We'll be talking about a few of these later.

Before we get too deep into day trading, let's look at some of the winning points that make day trading such an attractive option.

Why Day Trade?

There are a few reasons day trading is such an attractive option for investors. First of all, you get to make money in ways that other investments simply can't offer. Stock prices don't usually fluctuate on an hourly basis, but they can with day trading. By day trading, you get to profit from the daily highs and lows of a stock. You can also use this to your advantage with options and forex trading strategies.

Another reason day trading is so attractive is because it's relatively easy to learn how to do it well. Many aspiring investors think that they have to quit their job and acquire years of expertise before they can get started with day trading. While these tactics do work for some, they're not necessarily the best way to start out.

You don't have to quit your job to start day trading, and this is an important point. You can learn the basics of day trading simply by going to a local broker and learning how to use their trading platform. This will allow you the ability to trade across a wide range of financial markets. Most brokerages offer real-time data, so you can see exactly what's happening in stocks, bonds and other assets around the world. Many brokers also offer customer service so you can ask questions and get answers right away.

There's a ton to learn about day trading, but you don't have to learn it all at once. The important thing is to get yourself set up, gain some hands-on experience and then adapt your skills as necessary.

Day Trading

Day trading is the demonstration of trading on the stock market during the day. Foreign countries are locked in with the exchange to publicize also. When we are hitting the sack, those nations that are awakening imply that there is a different side to the market that numerous individuals don't consider. In any case, for the time being, how about we worry about the nuts and bolts.

The key point of convergence of day trading is to purchase and offer a stock inside one day to make a benefit. This isn't the main technique for trading. Many day traders are doing this now with the internet. Internet trading is the same thing as trading in person. You get the same stocks, at the same prices, at the same time. That is why many people are moving out of the stock market and onto the internet. This is especially useful in day trading because it executes your purchases and sales instantly. When you are dealing with stocks that are moving fractions of a point, being able to complete a transaction immediately is extremely important. There are many places that you can get information to help you find the answer to what is day trading. Online sources can offer you a wealth of information. There are also trade schools that can help you get started. Many schools provide seminars. Some schools even offer all-day lessons that can get you caught up on all the latest stock market news, techniques, and trends.

If you should be a compelling seller, you need to get data about the market. The more information you have, the better your chances are to acquire money. It is a very complicated market, and you need to be tuned to the current market trends. Staying informed can help you when it comes time to make decisions about your stocks. Day trading can be a very lucrative activity if you know how to do it right. Why day trade? Is it worth the effort? Day exchanging offers the way to financial opportunity.

You shouldn't be incredibly keen to be successful in day exchanging. The best day traders are the individuals who have iron-resolve and robust order. Intelligence is unquestionably invited yet isn't a fundamental basis for progress. I was never the top in my group and consistently scratched through my tests. Exchanging takes an alternate way to deal with bring in money. The period considered is short from a couple of moments to hours to days, weeks, or perhaps a month. Day exchanging alludes to carefully transferring inside the day. This implies you don't hold positions for the time being. For example: if you buy at 10:00 (EST), you need to sell before 16:15(EST) when the market closes. There are no standards against holding, for the time being, nevertheless, the hazard is limited if exchanging is carefully confined to inside the day. The market regularly moves in response to the news when exchanges are shut. Stocks generally don't have a lot of liquidity and trade on light volume secondary selling hours. Envision what might befall your long position when there is a sudden tropical storm strike when the market is shut. The market will drop, yet you probably won't have the option to sell at a sensible price because of low volume. Whatever losses and rewards are exacting during market hours when there is enough volume to trade.

Trading in Stocks

The thought of trading in stocks scares away many investors. Individuals who have never traded are terrified by the fact that one can easily lose money with wrong decisions. The reality is, stock trading is a risky activity. However, when approached with the right market knowledge, it is an efficient way of building your net worth.

It is a financial instrument which amounts to ownership in a company. When an individual purchases a stock or shares, it means that they own a portion or fraction of the company. For instance, say a trader owns 10,000 shares in a company with 100,000 shares. This would mean that the individual has 10% ownership of the stakes. The buyer of such shares is identified as a shareholder. Therefore, the more shares one owns, the larger the proportion of the company which they own. Every time the value of the company shares rise, your share value will also rise. Similarly, if the value falls, your share value also declines. When a company makes a profit, the shareholders are also bestowed with the profits in the form of dividends.

Preferred stock and common stock are the two main types of stocks you should be aware of. The difference that lies between these stocks is that with common stocks, it carries voting rights. This means that a shareholder influences company meetings. Hence, they can have a say in company meetings where the board of directors is elected. On the other hand, preferred shares lack voting rights. However, they are identified as "preferred" shares or stocks because of their preference over common stocks. If a company goes through liquidation, shareholders with preferred shares will be preferred to receive assets or dividends.

Trading in Forex

Most traders would argue that trading in the forex is quite complicated. However, it's not. Just like any other form of trading, you must stick to the basic rules. In this case, you need to buy when the market is rising and ensure you sell when the market is dropping. Trading in forex involves the process of trading in currencies. In simpler terms, a trader exchanges currency for others based on certain agreed rates. If you have traveled to foreign countries and exchanged your currency against their local currencies, you should understand how trading in forex works.

At first, it could seem confusing to choose the best currencies, but a trader should simply go for major currencies. Some of the frequently traded currencies include the U.S. dollar, Japanese Yen, European Union Euro, Australian dollar, Canadian dollar, and Swiss franc. An important thing you ought to understand about forex trading is that you need to trade in pairs. This means that when you are buying one currency, you should do this while simultaneously selling another. If you do some digging, you will notice that currencies are quoted in pairs, i.e.,

USD/JPY or EUR/USD. Below is an image showing how currencies are quoted in pairs.

Trading in Futures

Also, others are discouraged from trading in futures because they think that it is difficult. Well, to some extent, this is true. Comparing trading in futures to trading in stocks, the former is very risky. There are different forms of futures contracts, including currencies, energies, interest rates, metals, food sector futures, and agricultural futures. The best futures contract you will find in the market are briefly in the following lines:

- **S&P 500 E-mini:** Most traders will fancy the idea of trading in the S&P 500 E-mini because of its high liquidity aspect. It also appeals to most investors because of its low day trading margins. You can conveniently trade in S&P 500 E-mini around the clock, not to mention that you will also benefit from its technical analysis aspect. Essentially, the S&P 500 E-mini is a friendly contract since you can easily predict its price patterns.

- **10 Year T-Notes:** 10 Year T-Notes is also ranked as one of the best contracts to trade-in. Considering its sweet maturity aspect, most traders would not hesitate to trade in this futures contract. There are low margin requirements that a trader will have to meet when trading in 10 Year T-Notes.

- **Crude Oil:** Crude oil also stands as one of the most popular commodities in futures trading. It is an exciting market because of its high daily trading volume of about 800k. Its high volatility also makes the market highly lucrative.

- **Gold:** This is yet another notable futures contract. It might be expensive to trade in gold, however, it is a great hedging choice more so in poor market conditions.

- **Trading in Stock Options:** Trading in stock options is almost like trading in futures. Here, a trader also buys stocks at a pre-established price and later sells when prices rise.

- **Capital Requirements:** Stock options trading also affected by the Pattern Day Trading Rule. This means that your minimum capital requirements will be $25,000. If you engage in more than four trades in a week, you should have about $30,000 in your trading account.

- **Leverage:** Since there are many options to choose from, leverage will vary. The exciting aspect of stock options is that they have high leverage amounts.

- **Liquidity:** Regarding liquidity, stock options are not that liquid. A keen eye on this market reveals that a few options are traded regularly. The low volume of trades is affected by the many options that traders can choose from. Fortunately, stock options are rarely manipulated by the market. Their values are not influenced by supply and demand.

- **Volatility:** Stock options are highly volatile.

From the look of things, stock options have similar pros and cons, like trading in stocks. Most new traders will shy away from this form of day trading due to its high capital demands. Its high volatility could be scary to most investors as it makes the market to be unpredictable. This makes this form of trading to be very risky. Therefore, it is not recommended for new traders.

Day trading charts and patterns

Charts are used by traders to monitor price changes. These changes determine when to enter or exit a trading position. There are several charts used in day trading. Although these charts differ in terms of functionality and layout, they typically offer the same information to day traders.

Some of the most common day trading charts includes:

1.   Line charts

2.   Bar charts

3.   Candlestick charts

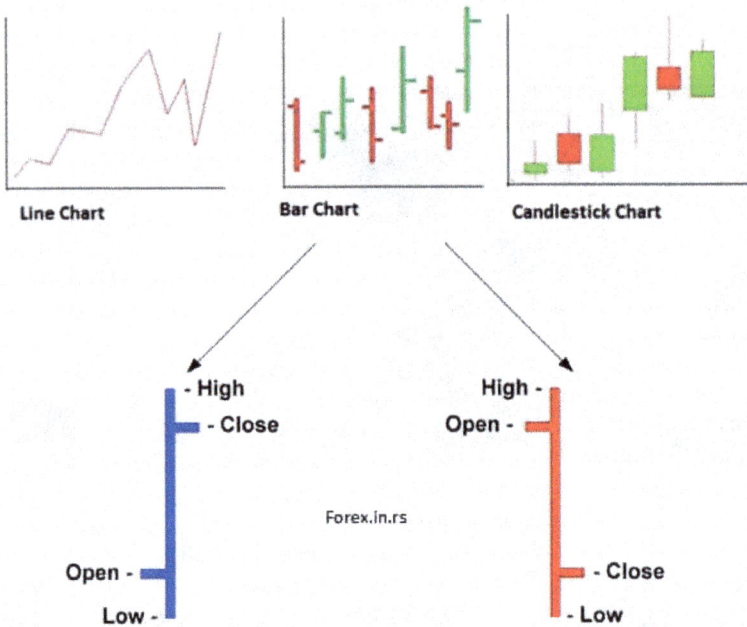

For each of the above charts, you must understand how they work as well as the advantages/ disadvantages involved.

Line Charts

These are very popular in all kinds of stock trading. They do not give the opening price, just the closing price. You are expected to specify the trading period for the chart to display the closing price for that period. The chart creates a line that connects closing prices for different periods using a line.

Most day traders use this chart to establish how the price of a security has performed over different periods. However, you cannot rely on this chart as the only information provider when it comes to making some critical trading decisions. This is because the chart only gives you the closing price. This means that you may not be able to establish other vital factors that have contributed to the current changes in the price.

Bar Charts

These are lines used to indicate price ranges for a particular stock over time. Bar charts comprise vertical and horizontal lines. The horizontal lines often represent the opening and closing costs. When the closing price is greater than the opening price, the horizontal line is always black. When the opening price is higher, the line becomes red.

Bar charts offer more information than line charts. They indicate opening prices, highest and lowest prices as well as the closing prices. They are always easy to read and interpret. Each bar represents rice information. The vertical lines indicate the highest and lowest prices attained by a particular stock. The opening price of a stock is always shown using a small horizontal line on the left of each vertical line. The closing price is a small horizontal line on the right.

Interpreting bar charts is not as easy as interpreting line charts. When the vertical lines are long, it shows that there is a significant difference between the highest price attained by a security and the lowest price. Large vertical lines, therefore, indicate that the commodity is highly volatile while small lines indicate slight price changes. When the closing price is far much higher than the opening price, it means that the buyers were more during the stated period. This indicates likelihood for more purchases in the future. If the closing price is slightly higher than the purchase price, then very little purchasing took place during the period. Bar chart information is always differentiated using color codes. You must, therefore, understand what each color means as this will help you to know whether the price is going up or down.

Advantages of bar charts

- They display a lot of data in a visual format

- They summarize large amounts of data

- They help you to estimate important price information in advance

- They indicate each data category as a different color

- Exhibit high accuracy

- Easy to understand

Disadvantages

- They need adequate interpretation

- Wrong interpretation can lead to false information

- Do not explain changes in the price patterns

Tick charts

Tick charts are not common in day trading. However, some traders use these charts for various purposes. Each bar on the chart represents numerous transactions. For instance, a 415 chart generates a bar for a group of 415 trade positions. One great advantage of tick charts is that they enable traders to enter and exit multiple positions quickly. This is what makes the charts ideal for day traders who transact volumes of stock each day.

These charts work by completing several trades before displaying a new bar. Unlike other charts, these charts work depending on the activity of each transaction, not on time. You can use them if you need to make faster decisions in your trade. Another advantage of tick chart is that you can customize each chart to suit your trading needs. You can apply the chart on diverse transaction sizes. The larger the size, the higher the potential of making a profit from the trade.

When used in day trading, tick hart works alongside the following three indicators:

- RSI indicators – these are used when trading highly volatile securities. They help you establish when a particular security is oversold or overbought since these are the periods when stock prices change significantly.

- Momentum – day traders use this together with tick charts to show how active the stock price is and whether the activity is genuine or fake. If the price rises significantly, yet the momentum is the same, this indicates a warning sign. Stocks with positive momentum are ideal for long trades. You should avoid these if you wish to close your positions within a day.

- Volume indicators – these are used to confirm the correct entry and exit points for each trade. Large trading positions are often indicated using larger volume bars while low positions with little volatility are displayed using small volume bars.

Candlestick Charts

Candlestick charts are used on almost every trading platform. These charts carry a lot of information about the stock market and stock prices. They help you to get information about the opening, closing, highest, and lowest stock prices on the market. The opening price is always indicated as the first bar on the left of the chart, and the closing price is on the far right of the chart. Besides these prices, the candlestick chart also contains the body and wick. These are the features that differentiate the candlestick for other day trading charts.

One great advantage of candlestick charts entails the use of different visual aspects when indicating the closing, opening, highest, and lowest stock prices. These charts compute stock prices across different time frames. Each chart consists of three segments:

- The upper shadow
- The body
- The lower shadow

The body of the chart is often red or green in color. Each candlestick is an illustration of time. The data in the candlestick represents the number of trades completed within the specified time. For instance, a 10-minute candlestick indicates 10 minutes of trading. Each candlestick has four points, and each point represents a price. The high point represents the highest stock price while low stands for the lowest price of a stock. When the closing price is lesser than the opening price, the body of the candlestick will be red in color. When the closing price is higher, the body will be colored green.

There are several types of candlesticks that you can use in day trading. One is the Heikin-Ashi chart that helps you to filter any unwanted information from the chart data, ending up with a more accurate indication of the market trend. Novice day traders commonly use this chart because of how clear it displays information.

The Renko chart only displays the changes in time. It does not give you any volume or time information. When the price exceeds the highest or lowest points reached before, the chart displays it as a new brick. The brick is white when the price is going up and black when the price is declining.

Lastly, the Kagi chart is used when you want to follow the direction of the market quickly. When the price goes higher than preceding prices, the chart displays a thick line. When the price starts to decline, the line reduces in thickness.

Each of the above charts works using a time frame which is represented using the X-axis. This time frame always indicates the volume of information represented by the chart. Time frames can be in the form of standard time or in the form of the number of trades completed within a specified period as well as the price range.

Day trading technical analysis

What is technical analysis?

Day trading is the buying and selling of financial instruments (e.g., shares, commodities) over a short period of time in order to profit from short-term price movement. Technical analysis is a set of rules designed to identify trends in financial markets by analyzing historical price data. So, what does this have to do with day trading? Chances are you're using the rules underlying technical analysis to make trades, whether you know it or not.

The process of technical analysis

A popular approach to technical analysis is the use of charts to visualize historical data. A common chart that's used by many traders is a candlestick chart. Candlesticks are my favorite visualization for day trading. Each candlestick represents some trading period, e.g., a day. Each day on a candlestick chart corresponds to a trading period. The same candlestick is used to represent that period in all candlestick charts. A line shows the open and close of each trading day. The lower end of the line is always close to zero and indicates us the beginning of each period, e.g., opening bell. The middle of the line is zero and represents the closing time for each trading day. The upper end of the line represents the last price for each period, e.g., closing bell.

Each candlestick represents a trading day (the red ones are my trades) on a candlestick chart, and you can use these to plot other things like MACD, trend lines, moving averages and even support and resistance levels. You might also typcially see Fibonacci levels, which are a tool used in technical analyses. Fibonacci levels show support and resistance areas based on the ratio of the area below a certain price to the area above it. Look at these lines as if they were drawn with invisible ink; when you can see through them, you're out of that area. Try to remember that technical analysis is just a tool, not all tools for all trades.

What should I be looking for?

Technical analysis is an ever-changing process. Prices are constantly moving, and changes will occur over time. This makes technical analysis an ever-changing process as well.

Now that you know some basic information about candlesticks, here are some examples of candlesticks and other techniques. They look like this:

The chart above represents a period of low volatility, or at least it appears that way based on the price history. We can also see that price moved up and down quite rapidly over the period. We might also notice that the stock reached a significant peak on February 20th, the open of this chart, and fell down from there. The stock eventually made another high on March 20th, which is represented by the red candlestick. It's important to note that this does not necessarily mean we should be trading today. We might just as well use a different time period than one-month, or use other methods to find our answer. The point is that each person will use different tools to come to a decision, but the answer is the same for everyone.

This second chart contains more information that we can take into consideration for our analysis. The chart above represents a period of high volatility. We can see price moving well beyond 2% on many days

DAY TRADING
STRATEGIES

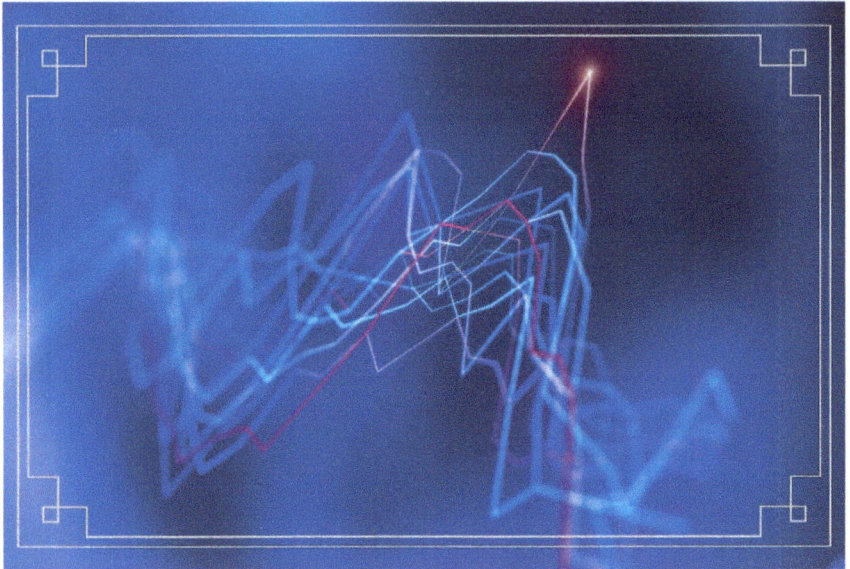

Day trading is not simple at first. Skills have to be built and some policies are set. All in all, it is a learning process that calls for patience and perseverance. Let us look at various fields at how you can get motivated this good day.

Day Trading Strategies for Beginners

- Financial analysis: Well, money is a very important asset. With that in mind, you need to be super careful in how you plan on using it. Failing to plan is planning to fail. Beginners are advised to use just a little amount of capital for a start-up until the time they are fully experienced in the day trading track. Most of the traders do not have more than 2% of the capital in the trade. Furthermore, as a beginner always consider slow but sure steps. Get to grow little by little. This is a journey with lots and lots of protocols to learn and master with a successful and rich endpoint.

- Seek every kind of learning material: Learning makes you educated on what you are actually doing. It makes you informed, you get to learn every living trick in that particular field (day trading). Take each day as a learning day in that you get to learn something new in a particular section. You get to grow. Being involved in day trading is a course journey itself. Below are some sources of learning materials for day trading:

- Videos: Videos provide practical learning sources and that is why they end being so famous. Explore several video learning contents from sites like YouTube.

- Articles, blogs, etc.: Day traders from different places of the world like to engage their experiences from the moment they started trading. As a beginner, seek the beginner level kind of sources. Read their experiences widely, take down important facts, and ask questions, recommendations. With that, even the confidence and the thrust force to begin day trading will highly be enlightened.

- Trends: Get to follow each and every trend and get the idea of what is actually happening. They are highly educative when it comes to future prediction analysis.

- Consistency or stability: Another idea to add, day trading is quite logical. Day trading cannot be analyzed by fear or even greed. Mathematical approaches have to be considered. Set strategies have to be put in place too! Examine every logical operation bound to happen during day trading so as to possess certain clear stability. Once stability has been established, expect some big-time profit rates and an excellent reputation.

- Timing: The trading market becomes volatile every single trading day. Experienced traders have mastered the moves and so they are quite sure about what steps to take next once they get to read the structures. For beginners? Quite not sure of what move to take. A slow but sure protocol is fundamental too. As a beginner, do not be quite in a rush to predict. Take one or more time to examine every single trend and get your desired prediction. Do not be too slow though, you may end missing so much.

- Scalping: Scalping kind of strategy takes advantage of the small kind of prices that happen drastically during the day trading sessions. This kind of mechanism involves getting engaged so quickly and so fast and then leaving right away.

How to Reduce Losses when Day Trading?

Day trading is made up of both losses and wins. The odds of both occurrences happening during trading are so high. We do try our best to win and, in the end, we do win frequently but in the end, losses never miss too. Below are some the ways in which we can reduce losses in our day to day training activities:

Manage your risk.

Managing your risk at individual trade is so important. It is super advisable that on a single trade you should not risk above 1% of your balance in the account. Taking an account setup of $100, 000 then a trader should not stake more than $1,000 on single market trade. With this information principled out, there are zero chances that one-point loss risks the loss of everything.

Consider using limit orders.

The use of limit orders is applicable for buying and selling. While the sell limit order will be used to sell stocks once it is above or equal to limit price, buy limit order will purchase it when it is below.

Bottom line.

Traders should always understand when they have intentions to enter and/ or exit a trade before execution. By applying stop losses cautiously, a trader usually minimizes huge losses while avoiding the number of counts a trade is usually dumbed needlessly.

Setting up stop- losses and take- profit points.

A stop-loss is a point at which a trader has preset as a mechanism to stop his/ her losses by disposing the trade at a loss whereas take- profit point being inverse is the actual price point at which a trader will cash in on the trade taking the profit already acquired on the margin difference. A stop-loss occurs when a trader had experiences that had not been planned. The points are designed to curb the "give it a little time" mentality of trading while limiting the unintended losses before they rise higher. On the other hand, take- profits occurs when the additional upside is limited given some risks.

Establish a daily stopping point.

As you set up some general strategies, decide on how much you are willing to risk per everyday trading session. Remember if you make the choice to set your stopping point based on average trading performance, the amount of time you are expected to lose is higher over a span of period as you continue to learn and master new styles during everyday trading sessions.

Take a wide look at your expected return.

Implement the formula in several day trading occurrences and compare the output and get to select the ones with the highest profit expectation rates.

Put options.

Put options give you the chance to sell an underlying stock at a specified priced during or at the blink of expiration of a given option.

Planning your trades.

Plan the trade and trade the plan. So as to secure yourself as the winner in a certain war, it will cost you to prepare for that. Preparing basically means setting up some strategies, really good strategies that will clearly thrust you forward and generally excel at the end game. Outline realistic strategies and at the end plan for your trades.

Stock Day Trading

Day trading is actually not even stock investing. If you are going to be completely honest about it, day trading is simply looking at technical signals or use related developments that impact a stock. For example, when your stock research software tells you in real time that a huge amount of investors is just plowing into a stock, then this should give you a good idea that something is about to break lose. People are buying into the stock in very high volumes. What you would do then is take a position based on a resistance level and if the stock breaks past that resistance level, you lock into your position. You subsequently ride up the upward momentum made possible by the increasing volume of trades in that stock.

Now, keep in mind that this goes the other way as well. If your stock research software notifies you that a stock is being traded heavily and there is a heavy volume in sales, this is going to put a tremendous downward pressure on the stock. You then take a position at a certain support level and once that support level is breached; you lock in for a purchase, and you ride the stock down. Once it bottoms out, you later buy back your shares that you have sold short.

Day trading involves very brief periods of time. We are talking a day or less than a day. In fact, a lot of day traders are quickly in and out of a stock in a matter of hours. Given the fact that they trade in volume due to margin accounts, they can make quite a nice chunk of money by simply trading a small proportion or even half a percent movement in certain stocks.

Again, the whole point in day trading is not looking the stock and analyzing its industry significance, its future prospects, new products, industry positioning, so on and so forth. No. Day trading is all about looking at technical trading characteristics and making a judgment call as to where the market is going regarding certain stocks. You then lock in a position and afterward you either ride up the stock, or you ride it down.

TRAITS THAT WILL ENSURE YOU SUCCEED AS A DAY TRADER

So how can you ensure that you will be successful at day trading? And what does it take to be successful? There are 3 psychological quirks that will have an enormous impact on your day trading. As a day trader, we can face some troubling problems, and most of these are going to be ones that we do not even know we have. Some of our human characteristics will affect how we trade and, in the end, our bottom line. Although there are several that can affect us, the five most important and detrimental are listed below, with a breakdown of how they do affect us with our day trading. These can place a block in the way of us achieving the goals that we have set for our finances.

1. There Are Several Enemies That We Do Not Even Recognize and Most of It Is Ourselves

When you deal with day trading, there will be moments that we will err, and this can be fixed, but only if we analyze it and make attempts to adjust the err. If you have exited from a trade too early, you will find that by adjusting your criteria, you will be able to make a better decision. Make adjustments to this error by looking for an indicator that is different or takes a longer amount of time to make the trade. If your trading strategy is solid, but you still find yourself losing some money, you will need to examine yourself and the psychology that we apply to the solution. When dealing with your own inner workings, your view is often skewed due to being so personally connected. You may not have the ability to fix the problem that is creating the loss. Your true problem could be created by a clouded mindset that is biased at best. There may be some trivialities that are superficial, and they are creating the discrepancies within your trading ability. For example, you have a trading strategy but never stick to it. So, this person is on a continuous adjustment period, and nothing is working because it is not given the proper time to work nor the right amount of credit. By sticking with a strategy, you will be able to check your resolve for solving the equation.

Your success record will increase by applying one specific approach that has a solid framework and foundation.

2.   There Is Power in Awareness

Being aware of the possibilities that could be creating the issues will help us to adjust them later. By creating actions which we can adjust over time, we can begin to see how each action is creating loss and change the habits that are contributing to this loss. We will overcome the problems that arise and be able to eliminate these problems. Since there is no magic plan that will make everyone a winner, this is where knowing who you are and adjust non-serving traits will come in handy. Psychology states that by being aware of our pitfalls, we can adjust them and improve upon who we are. This rings true for the day trader as well. Changing our habits and creating a profit will help us to be better at our day trading.

3. Bias Sensory-Derived

By compiling information from the experiences around us, we gain opinions, and this can create a bias with which will dictate how we operate. This will allow the investor to function as well as learn behaviors. However, as we understand that this is forming behaviors or opinions that would be factual in bases and evidence shows, it is often not the case. For instance, a trader who watches the news and bases his knowledge on the reports will believe he has stripped the opinions from the broadcaster and is going on pure facts when he, in fact, is not. If our sources are all biased, then how can we expect our own thoughts and opinions not to be biased based. There are always two sides to every story, and biased is the basis with which these stories have differences.

Constant exposure to a biased opinion can, in turn, make you believe that this biased opinion is your own truth, even if it is not factual. Those raised to believe that dogs are scary will, no matter what, always believe that dogs are scary even if there are no bases for the truth. Since there is no counterevidence to dispute the bias, the opinion becomes their truth as it is the only available information that has heard, even if it is biased.

4. Vagueness and Ambiguity Are Avoided

This can also be known as the fear of the unknown. The avoidance of what is possible to occur, even if it has not. The avoidance of things that is not clear to our thoughts. This avoidance can prevent even a seasoned investor from doing things that would increase their profit line and keep them locked in that state of loss. Some traders have actually found that they fear the process of making money, and this rings true for many entrepreneurs as well.

This is not a conscious fear; it is something that is deep within. The fear of the taxes that they will owe can be so daunting that they will fear themselves into losses. Expanding the zone with which they are comfortable can create blocks and worry that sends them into downward spirals of loss. This creates patterns of sabotage that is done by self. This can also create a bias about which industry they will enter, making them fear trading in any other industry than the one they are most familiar with. The fact that this industry is declining will be irrelevant to them. They will simply continue to pump money into a dead horse. They avoid the chance of winning a profit by staying in familiar investments and associate this with uncertainty.

This can also be seen when the investor holds onto winners less time than they should and sells the loser way later than they should have. If the price fluctuates, they struggle to face the facts of the movement and then fail at determining the appropriate action. They also will fear the experience of loss and begin to make drastic and risky decisions that will place them in jeopardy of losing it all. When they deviate from the rational, they will then become irrational and start acting accordingly. This then causes the investor to miss the gains that potentially could make them increase their wealth.

5.   The Anticipation Is Tangible

Anticipation is immensely powerful and can create stress as well as worry and excitement. Since anticipation is connected to "I want" or "I need," the mentality is self-serving. Most of the time, our anticipations will take place way in the future, and sometimes, they will take place within a few weeks. Although these can be far in the future, they create an emotional enjoyment that becomes addicting. This addiction can become the focus of how we want to feel always, and this becomes the achievement instead of the reaction. This can limit our ability to see that the payout is now and block us from taking the payment with anticipation that there is a bigger one coming, and eventually, we lose the money altogether or make ways less than we should have. Easy money can find its way to our door.

It is more than likely that it will be grabbed by the ones that think calm and collected about their trading values. We can begin to fall into an anticipatory feeling that becomes the consolation and not the reaction to the prize. Watching the changing of hands for billions of dollars can be exciting, but if the confidence is not there, we can miss our opportunity to benefit from this changing of hands. This is like us subconsciously telling ourselves that we are better off dreaming and that this dream is better than the real thing. Wanting to become profitable has become the goal instead of actually being profitable. By understanding what is affecting our trading, we can begin to make changes for the better. The psychology of day trading can be an extensive research project in and of itself, but awareness of how we respond and what our actions are can bring us to understand better why we are at this point. One way to adjust our psychology is to remove the bias that is influencing our decisions.

Use charts, since they do not lie. Remain objective and become focused on the strategies that will bring profit instead of the movement of price. Avoid others' well-thought-out opinions and create some of your own. Gain knowledge of how the market moves and shakes. This will help you overcome the fear and the greed that will arise during a day trading career. Unknown territory can create mistakes, so avoid the unknown by researching and gaining knowledge. Base all of our actions on an objectively sound decision that is made with knowledge instead of fear.

SCALPING

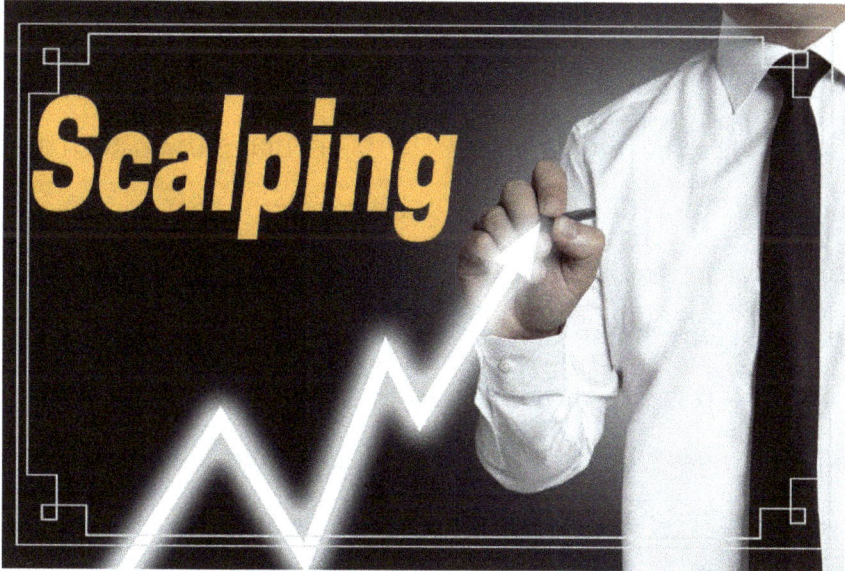

Basics of Scalping

Always remember that personality determines the trading style. You don't do what others are doing. You do what will match your trading personality, style, and approach. When you're a position trader, your system is designed to take a long-term view of assets. When you switch to a scalping trading, your system might be suitable with that mode of trading. However, a day trader can use scalping several times in a day. Generally, day trading involves holding positions for about thirty minutes or more. But scalping involves holding positions from seconds to even five minutes. That is why many scalpers love reading and analyzing five-minute stock charts. It helps them to make good scalping decisions. A scalper cannot wait for several days before trading. He or she is an active trader, looking to make the most amount of profit in the market in the shortest possible time. Thus, a scalper engages in more trades than all the others of traders in a single trading session. To get started with scalping, you need to understand the basics and how it works. Based on this definition, there are few things you must know: one, scalping focuses on "profiting off small price changes" and the second is that the seasoned scalpers simply focus on "a trade that has been executed and becomes profitable." They do not worry about huge price changes in the market. A scalper makes trading easy because they lavage profitable trades to make profits.

Types of Scalping

Volatility, pricing, and volume are the three main factors that influenced how scalp trades are being placed. Before you proceed and start using scalping, you might as well learn a lot from about these critical elements of successful scalping. Not only do they affect scalping, but they also help to create the different types of scalping that exit in the financial market.

- **Less Volatile Security" Approach:** This type of scalping focuses on trading fewer volatile stocks with no real price changes, but they have high trading volume. Once there is a large trading volume, scalpers will then focus on capitalizing the spread to trade and make profits. This type of scalping is known as "market-making."

In this approach, a scalper is trying to bet against the "market makers." It is executed by posting a bid and an offer on the same financial instrument simultaneously. You level the price difference between the bid and the offer to quickly make money in the market. Analyzing the direction of the stock and volume is critical for success.

- **"Highly Volatile Security" Approach:** When the stock or a financial instrument is quickly moving, you can consider a trading approach that will tally with the volatility of the market. When the market is volatile, pricing will obviously be changing quickly, creating a perfect environment for scalp trading.

The idea here is to buy many shares and the bet against price movement. When the price moves slightly, the scalp will generate a profit and you will win. The stock must be liquid, and you need to evaluate and time the market well before trading. The focus is to wait for a small movement to make a profit.

- **"Close at Exit" Approach:** In the third trading approach, you use the same or similar trading as the second one. You try to make profits by waiting for a small change in prices of stocks or financial securities to make money. But here, you're more focused on your exit. Once the trade hits your exit strategy, you close the trade, take your profits and get out of the position.

With this approach, you need to analyze and develop an exit strategy that allows you to make the maximum from the scalp as well as reduce losses from market reversals. Ideally, the risk/reward ratio for this kind of trade will be set at 1:1. A scalper operates with the belief that it is easy to capture profit from small prices changes in the financial market rather than wait for a large price moves to make a profit. The accumulated profits from the small profits are what give scalpers the winning edge over long-term traders like position traders. To become a successful scalper, you need to have a specific way of thinking, behaving and acting. If not, you will see yourself giving up before you succeed. No matter the kind of financial instrument you want to engage in through scalping, here are the top three psychological and behavioral patterns you must have.

- **Consistency:** Scalping can look very easy from the outside, but if you don't follow a trading system consistently, you're not going to make it. As a scalper, you're placing trades every few minutes and second.

That means your trading must be carefully planned and organized to avoid disaster. If you do not, you will only waste your trading capital on useless stuff.

- **Discipline:** The decision-making system of a scalper is quite different from that of a swing trader and a day trader. You need to be brutally hard with yourself to be successful. When you reach a decision about a trading decision, you don't have time to be feeling and rehearsing. You must learn to independent decisions very quickly to enter and exit a trade.

- **Flexible:** While you must be hard on yourself, rugged and stiff with your trading plan and system, you need to also be flexible. Flexibility is necessary to respond to change that might occur in the market that might not be discoursed in your trading plan. When a trade is not going as you expect, just get out of the market and move on to the next trade.

- **Commitment to research:** A position trader needs an amount of research to trade, but scalping needs more. If you're scalping, you are placing more trade in a day and that requires you to do your homework on different kinds of securities before scalping. By so doing, you can ensure that all you can construct your trade very well to be successful.

- **Trading Strategies for Scalpers:** Once you have chosen to use scalping to trade the financial market, you must familiarize yourself with the methods, ideas, and techniques required to be successful in the long term. This will ensure that you succeed. There are certain tools required for scalping. Some of them include a direct access broker, five minutes' chart and a live news feed and alert. All this is required for trading success.

Your scalping will always begin with preparation and market analysis. Since fundamental news about companies and economics has a bearing on the price, trend, and directions in the market; it will be very important that you get access to a news feed that can provide you with all this information.

Your job is to understand, and trade based on the news, that is news trading. Using fundamental ratios about the stock is also key in making good scalping decisions. These rations help you to figure out new supply and demand forces that will likely breakout after a major event.

But, most of the time, your scalping will heavily be dependent on technical analysis. Using short term historic price information to predict small changes in the market with the help of other technical indications such as moving average, candlestick charts, cups and handles, triangles, and trend channel. Consider volume and price spread before making the trading decisions. Always make sure volume and trend correlated together.

When you are trading with support and resistant indicators, the key is to look for low volatility and a high trading range. Low productivity helps to keep the market calm, avoid light price fluctuation that might work against your trade. Trading range, support and resistance levels will enable us to know where to enter and exit the market to make a profit.

What should be your risk management criteria?

Well, you can consider a risk/reward ratio of 1:1. This means you should have a target profit is as equal as the stop loss. You are risking as much as you are earning to make the trade successful because of the price length of the trade. Examining the trade and focusing on the right market indicators is the key. Unlike position trading, which works better in a bull market, you can execute scalp trades in both bull and bear market. The strategy in a bear market is to make a profit as prices go upward and the strategy in a bear market is to maximize profits from financial securities that do better in a bad market. You can use scalp trading for options, stocks, index, futures, and many others. It all depends on your strategy.

SWING TRADING

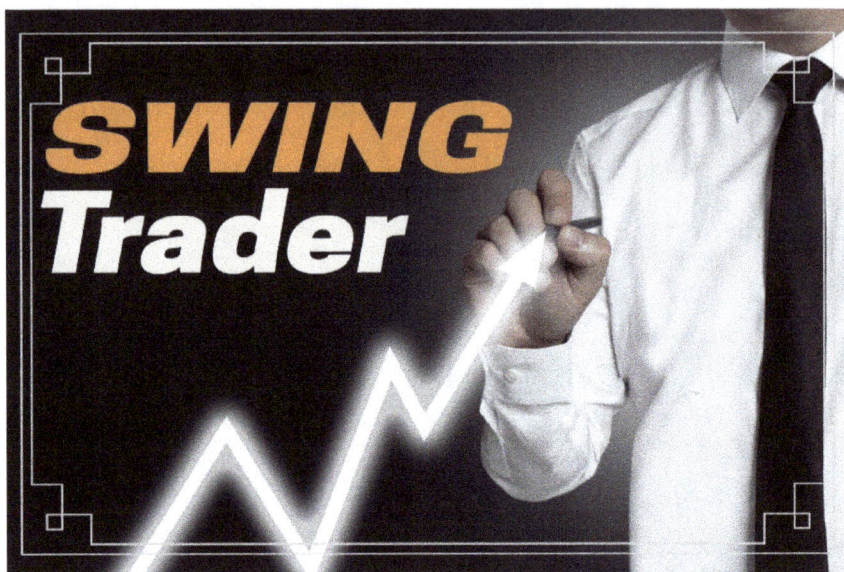

This is another form of short term trading, but with one major difference: swing trading doesn't necessarily have an expiration date in mind. In other words, a swing trader might have a trade open for a few days, a few weeks, or even months. Swing trading is much less risky than day trading because the trader doesn't have to worry about making trades on the same day or hour every day. It's more of an investment type of strategy.

The Winning Point is...

1. Always be prepared to take advantage of a trade setup.

Wait to react until you have identified and validated a possible trade set up, which will happen if your trading system has been working correctly and your risk management is in place.

2. Keep in mind that good trades don't always happen when expected, so be prepared for them at any time or day. 3.

Swing Trades are best taken when the market moves in a certain direction for a certain period of time.

4. The closer you are to the entry price, the more volatile & higher chances of success, so it's better to close trades closer to the initial entry price than it is to take trades out further from that price because you need more time.

5. Be aware of any trading system which stops taking advantage of Swing Trades after 5 or 6 consecutive wins.

6. Always trade using the Good Luck Principle.

7. The more you trade good wins and bad losses, the more your system will improve over time, so trading in this way is self-perpetuating.

8. Stay aware of the overall market sentiment and direction, so that you don't make 'Greater Losses' by entering trades during a strong uptrend or down trends.

Swing Trading

Just like many other aspiring swing traders, I bet you heard about swing trading, and you were instantly excited about the idea, your fingers are itching to try it out, but you have no idea how to start. Getting into swing trading can prove to be extremely difficult if you do not have the necessary skills and knowledge to succeed because most of the trader's encounter failure and consequently lose all their capital within the first year. You must come up with a strategy and then make sure that you have the discipline to work hand in hand with it. In the long run, you will emerge victorious where most people have failed.

Evaluate the Risks

Take a moment before you quit your job or choose to spend all your savings on swing trading to look at the disadvantages of swing trading. They include:

Market Risk

The first rule in swing trading is that the likelihood of losing your capital is significantly high. In as much as some people have made it appear easy, making any wrong move will be a pinch that you will feel in a very painful way, losing your capital. Unfortunately, the nature of the market has always been that lessons are usually learned the hard way. Also, using leverage as well as choosing to conduct your trade on a margin could lead you to encounter more losses than the investment you made.

Time

It is important to keep in mind that unlike other trades, swing trading is not one where you can get into your position and then disappear, only to reappear a week to check it. Swing trading is trading in real-time, and the truth is that strategies that prove to be successful require continuous monitoring. This insinuates that juggling a full-time job and swing trading may prove to be extremely challenging.

Taxes

Being a swing trader does not exempt you from paying taxes whatsoever. For instance, in the United States of America, you might get yourself entangled in the last of a pattern day trader. Therefore, make sure that you begin by taking care of any commitments or responsibilities in your financial system first.

Risk Management

Irrespective of whether your interest is in algorithm service or penny stocks, failing to put in place an efficient money and risk management plan could be very costly to you in the long run. Harry Lite, a successful trader, said that during his entire career in finance, he had constantly seen examples of numerous other traders that he had known being brought to their knees because they did not take risk options into consideration when they started off. If you do not kick risk out of the way, it will kick you.

Determine What Stocks to Trade

Probably one of the first tips or strategies you will be given in podcasts, user guides, and training videos is that you must select the appropriate securities. For example, in the case of stocks, large-cap stocks usually have the degree of volatility and volume that you need. Often, these stocks will move between serious highs and extreme lows. This insinuates that you can move towards one direction for a couple of days up to a point where you spot patterns of reversal, and then you can change to the alternate part of the trade. Selecting the appropriate stocks is a fundamental part of a swing trading plan. A valuable tip in that regard is that your choice of platform is based on effective scanner and screeners. There is basically no use putting in place the best trade plan if you are gambling on the inappropriate lowly priced stocks.

Choose the Right Market

Swing trading can prove to be extremely challenging regarding the two parts or divisions in the market. These are the bear market and raging bull market environment. Here, you will discover that even stocks that are highly active will not show similar downwards and upwards oscillations as it is usually the case whenever indices are somehow in a stable condition for months on end. You will instead find in a bull or bear market that there is a momentum that usually carries stocks for a long period of time in one direction. From this, you can conclude that the best point of entry, as well as the strategy, is the one that is usually on a long-term basis trend.

Basically, it is at this point where markets are not heading in any direction that you get the appropriate environment to swing trade. For instance, if it happens that you trade on NYSE, you will want the index to upsurge for several days and then decline for several days, after which the pattern is repeated. In as much as the stock might go back to its initial value after some months, you will have had multiple chances to capitalize and take advantage of the short-lived fluctuations.

Learn to Use the Exponential Moving Average (EMA)

If you happen to go to an institution that teaches swing trading, they will rush you through pivot points, gaps, technical indicators, and alerts. However, probably one of the major principles you will be taught is the exponential moving average.

Basically, this refers to a simple moving average, only that in this case, it increases its focus on the most recent data points. It is used in the right manner; it can assist you in identifying trend indicators and the points of entry and exit much faster in comparison to the simple moving average. Basically, you can utilize your exponential moving average to deduce your exit and entry plan.

Learn the Psychology of Swing Trading

The invention of the internet has made it easy for you to download numerous PDFs, audiobooks, and podcasts that will give you types of swing trading, regulations as well as charts to create. Nonetheless, what they usually miss telling you is the kind of mental reaction you should have if your plan does not work. You should consider the following tips:

Come up with a strategy and stick to it
It is almost guaranteed that there will be high moments as well as low moments because that is simply the nature of purchasing and selling in the trade. Nonetheless, let the numbers determine those high and low moments, but do not let your feelings get in the way. Making the decision to sell can rapidly turn into an emotional choice, especially if you have long-term returns at stake. Therefore, come up with a strategy and abide by it religiously.

Get the Right Broker and Exchange

Everybody has different priorities and needs, therefore, in as much as a trader swinging cryptocurrency may be well off on Binance or Gdax, a swing trader who may be extremely active in forex might want to opt for Dailyfx. Also, take note that brokers can be more than a place to get quotes and do security exchanges; they can assist you to come up with a diverse portfolio, watch list, and many more.

Make Use of the News

Markets are usually in continuous motion as a reaction to events in the news. Numerous resources like CNBC and Yahoo Finance will give market commentary and analysis using price action, weekly charts, and volume. Therefore, if used appropriately, the news could assist you to pinpoint dividend stock as well as potential options to monitor, for instance. It could also be instrumental in planning your point of entry and exit.

Never Stop Learning

The only path to achieve success from a trading point of view is to have an unquenchable, undying, and indefatigable thirst for knowledge and information. There are numerous sources of information to aid you in coming up with effective forex and cryptocurrency strategies. For instance, video tutorials can show you Gann skills as well as how to begin making use of weekly deep, especially in the case of money options.

Keep a Journal

Having the excel type of journal can turn out to be invaluable. What you can do is that you can just write down the date, position size, price, and a reason why you settled on the given points of entry and exit. This will help you figure out why your breakout strategy for currency pair is not applicable in weekly charts, for instance.

CONCLUSION

Before you start trading short-term, there are a few factors you should be aware of that can have a huge impact on your personal positions.

Short-term trading, in fact, has certain requirements in terms of technology because of the speed of execution needed to open and close positions quickly. In short-term strategies, fast execution can make the difference between profit and loss.

This is why it is important to use a platform that is specifically designed to ensure speed, stability and the best possible prices. Most platforms that offer a full experience come at a significant price, but there are also online trading platforms that are completely free.

The important thing is to choose the one that guarantees you adequate speed in executing your orders and gives you a guarantee of seriousness.

Our advice is to always practice on the demo platforms before starting with the real market.

Perhaps the most significant risk caused by slow execution is slippage. This occurs when the price at which the order is executed differs from the requested price. It happens in fast moving markets when one's broker is unable to execute the trade quickly enough to guarantee the requested price.

Some brokers fill the order at the new, and often worse, price. However, there are more serious brokers who implement the best execution policy which ensures that if the price moves outside of specific tolerance limits, they may reject an order to protect the client from slippage and give the client the option to choose to trade at the new price. These brokers, by the way, in the event of positive slippage (which occurs when the market price moves in favor of the client after the client has placed the order), will execute the trade at the best price for the client. Or, again, they offer the possibility of attaching a guaranteed stop to the client's position. In this way, the guaranteed stop is always executed at the price selected by the client, unlike what happens with normal stops, which are affected and influenced by slippage. Another advantage is that the premium is paid only if the guaranteed stop is activated.

This is yet another demonstration - and we never tire of repeating this to our clients and to those who ask us for advice - that the choice of the right broker makes the difference: the difference between a profitable trade and a riskier one.